VERSUS

Books by Ogden Nash

THE PRIMROSE PATH

GOOD INTENTIONS

THE FACE IS FAMILIAR
The selected verse of Ogden Nash

OGDEN NASH

VERSUS

LONDON
J. M. DENT & SONS LTD

J. M. DENT & SONS LTD.
Aldine House · Bedford St. · London

Printed in Great Britain
by
Lowe & Brydone Printers Ltd. London
First published in the U.S.A. 1949
First published in Great Britain 1949
Last Reprinted 1950

For

LINELL and ISABEL

with all my heart

Some of these verses have appeared in the following magazines and are reprinted through the courtesy of American Magazine, Cosmopolitan, '47, '48, Good Housekeeping, Harper's Bazaar, Ladies' Home Journal, McCall's, The New Yorker, Promenade, The Saturday Evening Post, Sport, and This Week.

CONTENTS

VERSUS

In far Tibet
There live a lama,
He got no poppa,
Got no momma,

He got no wife,
He got no chillun,
Got no use
For penicillun,

He got no soap,
He got no opera,
He don't know Irium
From copra,

He got no songs,
He got no banter,
Don't know Jolson,
Don't know Cantor,

He got no teeth,
He got no gums,
Don't eat no Spam,
Don't need no Tums.

He love to nick him
When he shave;
He also got
No hair to save.

Got no distinction,
No clear head,
Don't call for Calvert;
Drink milk instead.

He use no lotions
For allurance,
He got no car
And no insurance,

No Winchell facts,
No Pearson rumor
For this self-centered
Nonconsumer.

Indeed, the
Ignorant Have-Not
Don't even know
What he don't got.

If you will mind
The Philco, comma,
I think I'll go
And join that lama.

THE HUNTER

The hunter crouches in his blind
'Neath camouflage of every kind,
And conjures up a quacking noise
To lend allure to his decoys.
This grown-up man, with pluck and luck,
Is hoping to outwit a duck.

THOUGHTS THOUGHT AFTER A
BRIDGE PARTY

All women are pets,

But most women shouldn't be allowed to open a package of cigarettes.

I call down blessings on their bonny heads,

But they can't open a package of cigarettes without tearing it to shreds.

Of the two sexes, women are much the subtler,

But the way they open a package of cigarettes is comparable to opening a bottle of wine by cracking it on the butler.

Women are my inspiration and my queen,

But as long as they can rip the first cigarette from the package they don't care what happens to the other nineteen.

Women are my severest friend

But the last nineteen cigarettes in packages opened by them are not only bent but sere and withered and the tobacco is dribbling out at either end.

Women are creatures of ingenuity and gumption,

Which is why when they finish one cigarette they leave the mutilated nineteen cigarettes for some man and go to work on a fresh package, thus leaving thirty-eight mutilated cigarettes for masculine consumption.

Women are ethereal beings, subsisting entirely on

chocolate marshmallow nut sundaes and cantaloupe,
But they open up a package of cigarettes like a lioness
opening up an antelope.

As I was wandering down the street
With nothing in my head,
A sign in a window spoke to me
And this is what it said:

"Are your pillows a pain in the neck?
Are they lumpy, hard, or torn?
Are they full of old influenza germs?
Are the feathers thin and forlorn?
Bring 'em to us,
We do the trick;
Re-puff,
Replenish,
Re-curl,
Re-tick,
We return your pillows, spanned-and-spicked,
Re-puffed, replenished, re-curled, re-ticked."

As I was wandering down the street
With too much in my head,
The sign became a burning bush,
And this is what it said:

"Is the world a pain in the neck?
Is it lumpy, hard, or torn?
Is it full of evil ancestral germs
That were old before you were born?
Bring it to us,

We do the trick,
Re-puff,
Replenish,
Re-curl,
Re-tick,
In twenty-four hours we return the world
Re-puffed, replenished, re-ticked, re-curled."

As I was wandering down the street
I heard the trumpets clearly,
But when I faced the sign again
It spoke of pillows merely.
The world remains a derelict,
Unpuffed, unplenished, uncurled, unticked.

Now the frost is on the pane,
Rugs upon the floor again,
Now the screens are in the cellar,
Now the student cons the speller,
Lengthy summer noon is gone,
Twilight treads the heels of dawn,
Round-eyed sun is now a squinter,
Tiptoe breeze a panting sprinter,
Every cloud a blizzard hinter,
Squirrel on the snow a printer,
Rain spout sprouteth icy splinter,
Willy-nilly, this is winter.

Summer-swollen doorjambs settle,
Ponds and puddles turn to metal,
Skater whoops in frisky fettle,
Golf-club stingeth like a nettle,
Radiator sings like kettle,
Hearth is popocatapetl.

Runneth nose and chappeth lip,
Draft evadeth weather strip,
Doctor wrestleth with grippe
In never-ending rivalship.
Rosebush droops in garden shoddy,
Blood is cold and thin in body,
Weary postman dreams of toddy,
Head before the hearth grows noddy.

On the hearth the embers gleam,
Glowing like a maiden's dream,
Now the apple and the oak
Paint the sky with chimney smoke,
Husband now, without disgrace,
Dumps ash trays in the fireplace.

There are several people who I can claim I am glad
    I am not, without being accused of pride and
    effrontery,
And one of them is the bartender of a French res-
    taurant in an English-speaking country.
The conversation of the customers isn't calculated to
    keep a bartender young,
Even when they converse in their mother tongue;
How much more dispiriting it must be when after the
    second Martini
They request a third because the first two are, not
    finished, but finis.
They select a Maryland, or cigarette,
And instead of Gotta light? it is Avez-vous une
    allumette?
When they cry Garçon after the school of Stratford
    atte Bowe or New Rochelle or Nineveh,
It is moot whether they want the waiter or Mrs.
    Minniver.
Somehow, in a bistro, or French eatery,
Everybody suddenly discovers they can talk like Sasha
    Guitry,
But they really can't,
And if I were the bartender I should poke them in the
    œil with the plume de ma tante.

STAG NIGHT, PALEOLITHIC

Drink deep to Uncle Uglug,
That early heroic human,
The first to eat an oyster,
The first to marry a woman.

God's curse on him who murmurs
As the banquet waxes moister,
"Had only he eaten the woman,
Had only he married the oyster!"

Listen, children, if you'll only stop throwing peanuts
and bananas into my cage,
I'll tell you the facts of middle age.
Middle age is when you've met so many people that
every new person you meet reminds you of some-
one else,
And when golfers' stomachs escape either over or under
their belts.
It is when you find all halfbacks anthropoidal
And all vocalists adenoidal.
It is when nobody will speak loud enough for you to
hear,
And you go to the ball game and notice that even the
umpires are getting younger every year.
It's when you gulp oysters without bothering to look
for pearls,
And your offspring cannot but snicker when you refer
to your classmates as boys and your bridge partners
as girls.
It is when you wouldn't visit Fred Allen or the Aga
Khan if it meant sleeping on a sofa or a cot,
And your most exciting moment is when your shoelace
gets tangled and you wonder whether if you yank
it, it will come clean or harden into a concrete
knot.
Also, it seems simpler just to go to bed than to replace a
fuse,

Because actually you'd rather wait for the morning paper than listen to the eleven o'clock news,

And Al Capone and Babe Ruth and Scott Fitzgerald are as remote as the Roman emperors,

And you spend your Saturday afternoons buying wedding presents for the daughters of your contemporers.

Well, who wants to be young anyhow, any idiot born in the last forty years can be young, and besides forty-five isn't really old, it's right on the border;

At least, unless the elevator's out of order.

WHO DID WHICH?

or

WHO INDEED?

Oft in the stilly night,
When the mind is fumbling fuzzily,
I brood about how little I know,
And know that little so muzzily.
Ere slumber's chains have bound me,
I think it would suit me nicely,
If I knew one tenth of the little I know,
But knew that tenth precisely.

O Delius, Sibelius,
And What's-his-name Aurelius,
O Manet, O Monet,
Mrs. Siddons and the Cid!
I know each name
Has an oriflamme of fame,
I'm sure they all did something,
But I can't think what they did.

Oft in the sleepless dawn
I feel my brain is hominy
When I try to identify famous men,
Their countries and anno Domini.
Potemkin, Pushkin, Ruskin,
Velásquez, Pulaski, Laski;
They are locked together in one gray cell,
And I seem to have lost the passkey.

O Tasso, Picasso,
O Talleyrand and Sally Rand,
Elijah, Elisha,
Eugene Aram, Eugène Sue,
Don Quixote, Donn Byrne,
Rosencrantz and Guildenstern,
Humperdinck and Rumpelstiltskin,
They taunt me, two by two.

At last, in the stilly night,
When the mind is bubbling vaguely,
I grasp my history by the horns
And face it Haig and Haigly.
O, Austerlitz fought at Metternich,
And Omar Khayyam wrote *Moby Dick*,
Blücher invented a kind of shoe,
And Kohler of Kohler, the Waterloo;
Croesus was turned to gold by Minos,
And Thomas à Kempis was Thomas Aquinas.
Two Irish Saints were Patti and Micah,
The Light Brigade rode at Balalaika,
If you seek a roué to irk your aunt,
Kubla-Khan but Immanuel Kant,
And no one has ever been transmogrified
Until by me he has been biogrified.

Gently my eyelids close;
I'd rather be good than clever;
And I'd rather have my facts all wrong
Than have no facts whatever.

Doctors tell me that some people wonder who they are,
    they don't know if they are Peter Pumpkin-eater
    or Priam,
But I know who I am.
My identity is no mystery to unravel,
Because I know who I am, especially when I travel.
I am he who lies either over or under the inevitable
    snores,
I am he who the air conditioning is in conflict with
    whose pores,
I am he whom the dear little old ladies who have left
    their pocketbooks on the bureau at home invari-
    ably approach,
And he whom the argumentative tippler oozes in be-
    side though there are thirty empty seats in the
    coach.
I am he who finds himself reading comics to some-
    body else's children while the harassed mother
    attends to the youngest's needs,
Ending up with candy bar on the lapel of whose previ-
    ously faultless tweeds.
I am he in the car full of students celebrating victory
    with instruments saxaphonic and ukulelean,
And he who, speaking only English, is turned to for
    aid by the non-English-speaking alien.
I am he who, finding himself the occupant of one Pull-
    man space that has been sold twice, next finds him-
    self playing Santa,

Because it was sold the second time to an elderly in-
    valid, so there is no question about who is going
    to sit in the washroom from Philadelphia to Atlanta.
I guess I am he who if he had his own private car
Would be jockeyed into sharing the master bedroom
    with a man with a five-cent cigar.

*Indoors or out, no one relaxes
In March, that month of wind and taxes,
The wind will presently disappear,
The taxes last us all the year.*

WHAT TO DO UNTIL THE DOCTOR GOES

or

IT'S TOMORROW THAN YOU THINK

Oh hand me down my old cigar with its Havana wrap-
    per and its filling of cubeb,

Fill the little brown jug with bismuth and paregoric,
    and the pottle and cannikin with soda and rhu-
    beb,

Lend me a ninety-nine piece orchestra tutored by
    Koussevitsky,

I don't want the ownership of it, I just want the usevit-
    sky,

Bring me a firkin of Arkansas orators to sing me ora-
    torios,

Remove these calf-clad Spenglers and Prousts and re-
    place them with paper-covered Wodehouses and
    Gaboriaus,

Wrap up and return these secretarial prunes and prisms,

Let me have about me bosoms without isms.

Life and I are not convivial,

Life is real, life is earnest, while I only think I am real,
    and know I am trivial.

In this imponderable world I lose no opportunity

To ponder on picayunity.

I would spend either a round amount or a flat amount

To know whether a puma is only tantamount to a cata-
    mount or paramount to a catamount,

It is honey in my cup,

When I read of a sprinter sprinting the hundred in ten
     seconds flat, to think: Golly, suppose he stood up!
I guess I am not really reprehensible,
Just dispensable.

For years we've had a little dog,
Last year we acquired a big dog;
He wasn't big when we got him,
He was littler than the dog we had.
We thought our little dog would love him,
Would help him to become a trig dog,
But the new little dog got bigger,
And the old little dog got mad.

Now the big dog loves the little dog,
But the little dog hates the big dog,
The little dog is eleven years old,
And the big dog only one;
The little dog calls him Schweinhund,
The little dog calls him Pig-dog,
She grumbles broken curses
As she dreams in the August sun.

The big dog's teeth are terrible,
But he wouldn't bite the little dog;
The little dog would grind his spine,
But the little dog has no teeth;
The big dog is acrobatic,
The little dog is a brittle dog;
She leaps to grip his jugular,
And passes underneath.

The big dog clings to the little dog
Like glue and cement and mortar;

The little dog is his own true love;
But the big dog is to her
Like a scarlet rag to a Longhorn,
Or a suitcase to a porter;
The day he sat on the hornet
I distinctly heard her purr.

Well, how can you blame the little dog,
Who was once the household darling?
He romps like a young Adonis,
She droops like an old mustache;
No wonder she steals his corner,
No wonder she comes out snarling,
No wonder she calls him Cochon
And even Espèce de vache.

Yet once I wanted a sandwich,
Either caviar or cucumber,
When the sun had not yet risen
And the moon had not yet sank;
As I tiptoed through the hallway
The big dog lay in slumber,
And the little dog slept by the big dog,
And her head was on his flank.

ON WAKING TO THE THIRD RAINY
MORNING OF A LONG WEEK END

Well, what shall I do today?
Shall I spend the day in the hay?
Shall I cover my head with the sheet,
Or go downstairs and eat?

If I leave my cozy nest
I will meet a fellow guest,
Or, what would irk me most,
I would meet my hostess and host,
While, if I stay upstairs,
My troubles are mine, not theirs.

I refuse to play Lotto or euchre
For either love or lucre;
I'm tired of discussing the arts,
And I've got bursitis from darts.
I am sick of people appearing
To announce that it looks like clearing;
Of memoirs of links and turf,
And quotations from Bennett Cerf;
Of games with pencil and paper,
And the girl who does Ruth Draper.

Today it would be as well,
I think, to lurk in my cell.
I'll refuse to speak to outsiders,
And only make friends with spiders;

I'll count the cracks in the floor,
And the steps between window and door;
I'll identify several stars
At night as I peer through the bars,
And when pastimes like these I exhaust,
I'll memorize Paradise Lost.

In closing, I'll mention, dear Auntie,
That the food here is wholesome but scanty;
If you'll send me a pie, when I open it
I'll hope for a file and a rope in it.

Man is a glutton,
He will eat too much even though there be nothing
    to eat too much of but parsnips or mutton.
He will deprecate his paunch,
And immediately afterwards reach for another jowl or
    haunch.
People don't have to be Cassandras or Catos
To know what will happen to their paunches if they
    combine hot biscuits and strawberry shortcake and
    French fried potatoes,
Yet no sooner has a man achieved a one-pound loss
Than he gains two through the application to an old
    familiar dish of a new irresistible sauce.
Thus cooks aggravate men's gluttony
With capers and hollandaise and chutney,
They can take seaweed or pemmican
And do things to them in a ramekin,
Give them a manatee that has perished of exposure
And they will whip you up a casserole of ambrosia,
Which is why a man who digs his grave with his teeth's
    idea of life beyond the grave is definite,
There's a divine chef in it.
Men are gluttons,
And everybody knows it except tailors, who don't leave
    room enough at the edge to move over the buttons.

THE CHERUB

I like to watch the clouds roll by,
And think of cherubs in the sky;
But when I think of cherubim,
I don't know if they're her or him.

WHO CALLED THAT ROBIN
A PICCOLO PLAYER?

ROBINS GETTING LAZY. — Robins, now usually half tame and preferring suburban to forest life, have become stupid and lazy in many cases. — New York Daily Mirror

Hark hark the lark, no it is not a lark, it is a robin sing-
ing like a lark,

He is in disguise because he is now the target of a newspaper crusade like dirty books and vivisection and
the man-eating shark.

He has been termed lethargic and fat,

It is said of him that he would rather live in Greenwich
or Great Neck than in Medicine Hat,

It is rumored that at the Garden Club his wife once
met an author,

And that he himself prefers a California Colonial bunga-
low to the tepee of Hiawatha,

And wears nylon instead of buckskin hosen,

And buys his worms at a super-market, Cellophane-
wrapped, and frozen.

In fact, the implication couldn't be clearer

That he is the spit and image of a reader of the Mirror.

Well for heaven's sake, how far can this scurrilous name-
calling degenerate?

They are now attempting to besmirch a bird that I
venerate.

His breast may be red, that is true,

But his heart is red, white and blue;

And as for being lazy, I know one robin that held down
two jobs at once just so his younger brother (their

parents had passed away uninsured) could get to
be a transport pilot,
But if you mentioned it he was modest as a buttercup
or vilot,
And the only reason he himself wasn't making those
selfsame flights,
He had a bad head for heights.
If these editorial scandalmongers have to mong scandal
about birds, let them leave the robin alone and turn
their attention to the pelican;
It has an Oriental background and a triangular horny
excrescence developed on the male's bill in the
breeding season which later falls off without leaving trace of its existence, which for my money is
suspicious and un-Amelican.

THE OUTCOME OF MR. MACLEOD'S
GRATITUDE

When Thanksgiving came twice, who walked so proud
As that grateful optimist, Mr. MacLeod?
Things you and I would deeply deplore
MacLeod found ways to be grateful for,
And this was his conscientious attitude:
Double Thanksgiving, double gratitude.
Whatever happened, no matter how hateful,
MacLeod found excuses for being grateful.
To be grateful, he really strained his wits.
Had he hiccups?
He was grateful it wasn't fits.
Had he hives?
He was grateful it wasn't measles.
Had he mice?
He was grateful it wasn't weasels.
Had he roaches?
He was glad it wasn't tarantulas.
Did his wife go to San Francisco?
He was glad it wasn't Los Angeles.
Mrs. MacLeod, on the other hand,
Was always complaining to beat the band.
If she had the mumps she found it no tonic
To be told to be grateful it wasn't bubonic.
If the cook walked out she would scream like a mink
Instead of being grateful she still had a sink.
So she tired of her husband's cheery note

And she stuffed a tea tray down his throat.

He remarked from the floor where they found him re-
    clining,

"I'm just a MacLeod with a silver lining."

·I have recently been pondering the life expectancy
    which the Bible allots to man,
And at this point I figure I have worked my way
    through nine fourteenths of my hypothetical span.
I have been around a bit and met many interesting
    people and made and lost some money and ac-
    quired in reverse order a family and a wife,
And by now I should have drawn some valuable con-
    clusions about life.
Well I have learned that life is something about which
    you can't conclude anything except that it is full
    of vicissitudes,
And where you expect logic you only come across ec-
    centricitudes.
Life has a tendency to obfuscate and bewilder,
Such as fating us to spend the first part of our lives be-
    ing embarrassed by our parents and the last part
    being embarrassed by our childer.
Life is constantly presenting us with experiences which
    are unprecedented and depleting,
Such as the friend who starts drinking at three in the
    afternoon and explains it's only to develop a hearty
    appetite for dinner because it's unhealthy to drink
    without eating.
Life being what it is I don't see why everybody doesn't
    develop an ulcer,
Particularly Mrs. Martingale, the wife of a prominent
    pastry cook from Tulsa.

He had risen to fame and fortune after starting as a
    humble purveyor of noodles,
So he asked her what she wanted for her birthday and
    she said a new Studebaker and he thought she said
    a new strudel baker and she hated strudels.
So all I know about life is that it has been well said
That such things can't happen to a person when they
    are dead.

Two cows
In a marsh,
Mildly munching
Fodder harsh.
Cow's mother,
Cow's daughter,
Mildly edging
Brackish water.
Mildly munching,
While heron,
Brackish-minded,
Waits like Charon.
Two cows,
Mildly mooing;
No bull;
Nothing doing.

In this foolish world there is nothing more numerous
Than different people's senses of humorous,
And the difference between different sense of humors
Is as wide as the gap between shorts and bloomers.
This is what humor boils down unto —
Are you him who doeth, or him who it's done to?
If a friend is dogged by some awful hoodoo,
Why, naturally, he doesn't laugh, but you do;
If the puppy is ill on your new Tuxedo,
Why, naturally, you don't laugh, but he do.
Humor depends on the point of view,
It's a question of what is happening to who;
It's a question facing which I surrender,
It's also a question of What's your gender?
Strong men have squandered the best of their life
In trying to coax a smile from their wife.
I know a wag named Septimus Best;
His wife won't laugh at his merriest jest.
Under her bed he hides a skeleton;
He fills her bathtub with glue and gelatin;
He draws whiskers on pictures of Cleopatra,
And he's disrepectful to Frank Sinatra;
And she just sits in her gown of taffta
And refuses to smile, either during or afeter.
I guess a sense of humor is what
Husbands tell each other their wives haven't got.

WE WOULD REFER YOU TO OUR SERVICE
DEPARTMENT, IF WE HAD ONE

It fills me with elation
To live in such a mechanical-minded nation,
Surrounded not only by the finest scenery
But also the most machinery,
Where every prospect is attractive
And people are radioactive,
Reading books with show-how
Written by scientists with know-how.
Breathes there with soul so dead a fossil
Who never to himself hath said, Production is colossal?
Obviously civilization is far from a crisis
When the land teems with skilled craftsmen skillfully manufacturing gadgets and mechanical devices.
Millions of washing machines and electric refrigerators
Are shipped from the shipping rooms of their originators,
Streamlined dreamlined automobiles roll off the assembly lines in battalions and droves,
Millions of radios pour from the factories for housewives to listen to in the time they save through not having to slice their pre-sliced loaves,
So when everybody has a houseful and a garageful of mechanical perfection no one has any worries, but if you want a worry, I will share one,
Which is, Why is it that when seemingly anybody can

make an automobile or a washing machine, nobody can repair one?

If you want a refrigerator or an automatic can opener or a razor that plays "Begin the Beguine" you can choose between an old rose or lavender or blue one,

But after you've got it, why if anything goes wrong don't think you'll find anybody to fix it, just throw it away and buy a new one.

Oh well, anyhow here I am nearly forty-five,

And still alive.

FIRST LIMICK

An old person of Troy
In the bath is so coy
That it doesn't know yet
If it's a girl or a boy.

WHO TAUGHT CADDIES TO COUNT?

or

A BURNT GOLFER FEARS THE CHILD

I have never beheld you, O pawky Scot,
And I only guess your name,
Who first propounded the popular rot
That golf is a humbling game.
You putted perhaps with a mutton bone,
And hammered a gutty ball;
But I think that you sat in the bar alone,
And never played at all.

Ye hae spoken a braw bricht mouthfu', Jamie,
Ye didna ken ye erred;
Ye're richt that golf is a something gamie,
But humble is not the word.
Try arrogant, insolent, supercilious,
And if invention fades,
Add uppitty, hoity-toity, bilious,
And double them all in spades.

Oh pride of rank is a fearsome thing,
And pride of riches a bore;
But both of them bow on lea and ling
To the Prussian pride of score.
Better the beggar with fleas to scratch
Than the unassuming dub
Trying to pick up a Saturday match
In the locker room of the club.

The Hollywood snob will look you through
And stalk back into his clique,
For he knows that he is better than you
By so many grand a week;
And the high-caste Hindu's fangs are bared
If a low-caste Hindu blinks;
But they're just like one of the boys, compared
To the nabobs of the links.

Oh where this side of the River Styx
Will you find an equal mate
To the scorn of a man with a seventy-six
For a man with a seventy-eight?
I will tell you a scorn that mates it fine
As the welkin mates the sun:
The scorn of him with a ninety-nine
For him with a hundred and one.

And that is why I wander alone
From tee to green to tee,
For every golfer I've ever known
Is too good or too bad for me.
Indeed I have often wondered, Jamie,
Hooking into the heather,
In such an unhumble, contemptful gamie
How anyone plays together.

THERE WERE GIANTS IN THOSE DAYS

or

MAYBE THERE WEREN'T

When people bandy about bright sayings they like to
attribute them to celebrities celebrated for their
witticism,

Hoping thereby both to gain prestige and forestall
criticism.

Thus many people in London have had their disposi-
tions soured

By being cornered by other people and told stories attributed to Mr. Shaw or Noel Coward,

While over here, if people tell an anecdote either
hygienic or spotty,

Why, they attribute it to Dorothy Parker, only they
usually cozily refer to her as Dottie.

I have never heard an anecdote attributed to Millard
Fillmore, William Henry Harrison, or Rutherford
B. Hayes,

So let us respectfully attribute the following titbits to
their posthumous praise.

When Millard Fillmore was told he would have to sign
a legal paper before leaving on his vacation he said,
What do they think I am, President of the United
States, or an ambulance-chasing oaf?

But he signed it anyhow because he said affidavit was
better than no loaf,

And when William Henry Harrison faced a knotty

problem he didn't wonder what would Gerald K.
Smith or Earl Browder do,

He simply recounted the story of the two jealous Indian
ranees who met on elephant-back and one rance
stroked her coiffure and said, Here's a pretty
hair-do, and the other rance stroked her elephant
and said, Here's a pretty howdah-do;

And once when Rutherford B. Hayes found himself
losing at backgammon,

Why, he casually upset the board and asked, Did you
hear about Lord Louis Mountbatten, he asked a
soldier in Burma, Are you Indo-Chinese? And the
soldier said, No suh, I'se out-do' Alabaman.

Kindly do not attribute these anecdotes to the under-
signed,

Kindly attribute them to these three hitherto unsung
statesmen, who are dead and probably won't mind.

O Adolescence, O Adolescence,
I wince before thine incandescence.
Thy constitution young and hearty
Is too much for this aged party.
Thou standest with loafer-flattened feet
Where bras and funny papers meet.
When anxious elders swarm about
Crying "Where are you going?", thou answerest "Out,"
Leaving thy parents swamped in debts
For bubble gum and cigarettes.

Thou spurnest in no uncertain tone
The sirloin for the ice-cream cone;
Not milk, but cola, is thy potion;
Thou wearest earrings in the ocean,
Blue jeans at dinner, if out of shorts,
And lipstick on the tennis courts.

Forever thou whisperest, two by two,
Of who is madly in love with who.
The car thou needest every day,
Let hub caps scatter where they may.
For it would start unfriendly talk
If friends should chance to see thee walk.

Friends! Heavens, how they come and go!
Best pal today, tomorrow foe,

Since to distinguish thou dost fail
Twixt confidante and tattletale,
And blanchest to find the beach at noon
With sacred midnight secrets strewn.

Strewn! All is lost and nothing found.
Lord, how thou leavest things around!
Sweaters and rackets in the stable,
And purse upon the drugstore table,
And cameras rusting in the rain,
And Daddy's patience down the drain.

Ah well, I must not carp and cavil,
I'll chew the spinach, spit out the gravel,
Remembering how my heart has leapt
At times when me thou didst accept.
Still, I'd like to be present, I must confess,
When thine own adolescents adolesce.

Once there was a man named Mr. Palliser and he asked
his wife, May I be a gourmet?

And she said, You sure may,

But she also said, If my kitchen is going to produce a
Cordon Blue,

It won't be me, it will be you,

And he said, You mean Cordon Bleu?

And she said to never mind the pronunciation so long
as it was him and not heu.

But he wasn't discouraged; he bought a white hat and
The Cordon Bleu Cook Book and said, How about
some Huîtres en Robe de Chambre?

And she sniffed and said, Are you reading a cook book
for Forever Ambre?

And he said, Well, if you prefer something more Anglo-
Saxon,

Why suppose I whip up some tasty Filets de Sole
Jackson,

And she pretended not to hear, so he raised his voice
and said, Could I please you with some Paupiettes
de Veau à la Grecque or Cornets de Jambon
Lucullus or perhaps some nice Moules à la
Bordelaise?

And she said, Kindly lower your voice or the neighbors
will think we are drunk and disordelaise,

And she said, Furthermore the whole idea of your cook-

ing anything fit to eat is a farce. So what did
Mr. Palliser do then?

Well, he offered her Œufs Farcis Maison and Homard
Farci St. Jacques and Tomate Farcie à la Bayonne
and Aubergines Farcies Provençales, as well as
Aubergines Farcies Italiennes,

And she said, Edward, kindly accompany me as usual
to Hamburger Heaven and stop playing the fool,

And he looked in the book for one last suggestion and
it suggested Croques Madame, so he did, and now
he dines every evening on Crème de Concombres
Glacée, Côtelettes de Volaille Vicomtesse, and
Artichauds à la Barigoule.

I love coffee, I love tea,
I love the girls, but they're mean to me.
I love Saturday, I love Sunday,
But how could anyone ever love Monday?
Let's make a scientific analysis,
Let's diagnose this Monday paralysis.
Well, you've suffered an overdose of sunburn;
You must blister and peel before you un-burn.
For junk your muscles could all be sold for,
From engaging in games you are now too old for.
You're bloated from a diet of buns and hamburgers,
Chickenburgers, cheeseburgers, nutburgers, clamburgers.
Your hair may be brushed, but your mind's untidy,
You've had about seven hours' sleep since Friday,
No wonder you feel that lost sensation;
You're sunk from a riot of relaxation.
What you do on week ends, you claim to adore it.
But Monday's the day that you suffer for it.
That's why Labor Day is a red-letter news day —
Blue Monday doesn't come until Tuesday.

Two things I have never understood: first, the difference
    between a Czar and a Tsar,

And second, why some people who should be bores
    aren't, and others, who shouldn't be, are.

I know a man who isn't sure whether bridge is played
    with a puck or a ball,

And he hasn't read a book since he bogged down on a
    polysyllable in the second chapter of The Rover
    Boys at Putnam Hall.

His most thrilling exploit was when he recovered a
    souvenir of the World's Fair that had been sent
    out with the trash,

And the only opinion he has ever formed by himself
    is that he looks better without a mustache.

Intellectually speaking, he has neither ears to hear with
    nor eyes to see with,

Yet he is pleasing to be with.

I know another man who is an expert on everything
    from witchcraft and demonology to the Eliza-
    bethan drama,

And he has spent a week end with the Dalai Lama,

And substituted for a mongoose in a fight with a cobra,
    and performed a successful underwater appendec-
    tomy,

And I cannot tell you how tediously his reminiscences
    affect me.

I myself am fortunate in that I have many interesting

thoughts which I express in terms that make them come alive,

And I certainly would entertain my friends if they always didn't have to leave just when I arrive.

THE PORCUPINE

Any hound a porcupine nudges
Can't be blamed for harboring grudges.
I know one hound that laughed all winter
At a porcupine that sat on a splinter.

THERE'S NOTHING LIKE INSTINCT.
FORTUNATELY.

I suppose that plumbers' children know more about
     plumbing than plumbers do, and welders' children
     more about welding than welders,
Because the only fact in an implausible world is that
     all young know better than their elders.
A young person is a person with nothing to learn,
One who already knows that ice does not chill and fire
     does not burn.
It knows that it can read indefinitely in the dark and
     do its eyes no harm,
It knows it can climb on the back of a thin chair to
     look for a sweater it left on the bus without falling
     and breaking an arm.
It knows it can spend six hours in the sun on its first
     day at the beach without ending up a skinless beet,
And it knows it can walk barefoot through the barn
     without running a nail in its feet.
It knows it doesn't need a raincoat if it's raining or
     galoshes if it's snowing,
And knows how to manage a boat without ever having
     done any sailing or rowing.
It knows after every sporting contest that it had really
     picked the winner,
And that its appetite is not affected by eating three
     chocolate bars covered with peanut butter and
     guava jelly, fifteen minutes before dinner.
Most of all it knows

That only other people catch colds through sitting
    around in drafts in wet clothes.
Meanwhile psychologists grow rich
Writing that the young are ones parents should not
    undermine the self-confidence of which.

I live at the top of old West Chop
In a house with a cranky stove,
And when I swim I risk life and limb
On the pebbles that line the cove —
Where the waves wish-wash, and the foghorn **blows,**
And the blowfish nibble at your toes-oes-oes,
The blowfish nibble at your toes.

I lunch and sup on schrod and scup,
And once in a while on beans,
And the only news that I get to peruse
Is in last year's magazines —
Where the waves wish-wash, and the foghorn **blows,**
And the blowfish nibble at your toes-oes-oes,
The blowfish nibble at your toes.

When the sea gulls shout the lights go out,
And whenever the lights go on
I pursue the moth with a dusting cloth
Till the Bob White brings the dawn —
Where the waves wish-wash, and the foghorn **blows,**
And the blowfish nibble at your toes-oes-oes,
The blowfish nibble at your toes.

But when the breeze creeps through the trees
And the wee waves shiver and shake,
Oh, I wouldn't swap my old West Chop

For a sizzling Western steak —
I want to wish-wash where the foghorn blows,
And the blowfish nibble at your toes-oes-oes,
The blowfish nibble at your toes.

THE PEOPLE UPSTAIRS

The people upstairs all practice ballet.
Their living room is a bowling alley.
Their bedroom is full of conducted tours.
Their radio is louder than yours.
They celebrate week ends all the week.
When they take a shower, your ceilings leak.
They try to get their parties to mix
By supplying their guests with Pogo sticks,
And when their orgy at last abates,
They go to the bathroom on roller skates.
I might love the people upstairs wondrous
If instead of above us, they just lived under us.

THE STRANGE CASE OF THE RENEGADE
LYRIC WRITER

Once there was a lyric writer named Mr. Amazon,

And being a lyric writer he spent most of his days with
his pajamas on.

He loved people until they got interested in songwriting
and asked him, Which comes first, the lyrics or the
music?

And then he was less enthusic;

And also, since he wrote words for the music in musical
comedies,

Why, he noted a great similarity between singers and
the man-eating horses of Diomedes,

Because although the singers couldn't eat the tunes —
you could always recognize the tunes as Chopin's
or Rodgers's or Schumann's —

Well, they ate his lyrics the way the man-eating horses
of Diomedes ate humans.

He was always complaining that Gee whiz,

Some people had to swallow their own words but singers only swallowed his;

And he swore that if he ever met a female singer who
would pronounce his words he would offer her
his heart and hand and undying loyalty

And 12½ per cent of his royalty.

Then one day he heard a new female singer in rehearsal

And his feelings underwent a reversal.

Her enunciation was fabulous,

He heard every one of his rhymes, even the most poly-
  syllabulous;
So to show his admiration and confidence he wrote a
  new song especially for her, beginning "The Leith
  police releaseth us, releaseth us the police of Leith,"
And on opening night he sent her a perfect rose, but it
  seems she was a Spaniard and she sang the song
  with the rose between her teeth.
Mr. Amazon couldn't even distinguish a vowel,
It was like hearing a candidate with a loose tooth talking
  to a barber through a hot towel.
Mr. Amazon no longer writes lyrics, he writes radio
  commercials, because there is one fact on which he
  finally pounced:
When a writer rhymes sour stomach with kidney tubes
  it may not be prosody but boy, is it pronounced!

Had she told the dicks
How she got in that fix,
I would be much apter
To read the last chapter.

If my face is white as a newmade sail,
It's not that it's clean, it's simply pale.
The reason it's pale as well as clean:
I'm a shaken survivor of Hallowe'en.
The little ones of our community
This year passed up no opportunity;
You should have seen the goblins and witches;
At our expense, they were all in stitches.
They shook with snickers from warp to woof
When our doormat landed on the roof.
And take a look at our garden's format —
It now resembles the missing doormat.
The doorbell got torn out by the roots,
So our guests announce themselves tooting flutes.
Don't blame me if I wince or flinch,
They tore the fence down inch by inch.
Forgive me if I flinch or wince,
We haven't seen our mailbox since,
And we can't get into our own garage
Since they gave the door that Swedish massage.
All this perhaps I could forgive,
In loving kindness I might live,
But on every window they scrawled in soap
Those deathless lines, Mr. Nash is a dope.
At the very glimpse of a Jack-o'-lantern
I've got one foot on the bus to Scranton.
When Hallowe'en next delivers the goods,
You may duck for apples — I'll duck for the woods.

I sit in the dusk. I am all alone.
Enter a child and an ice-cream cone.

A parent is easily beguiled
By sight of this coniferous child.

The friendly embers warmer gleam,
The cone begins to drip ice cream.

Cones are composed of many a vitamin.
My lap is not the place to bitamin.

Although my raiment is not chinchilla,
I flinch to see it become vanilla.

Coniferous child, when vanilla melts
I'd rather it melted somewhere else.

Exit child with remains of cone.
I sit in the dusk. I am all alone,

Muttering spells like an angry Druid,
Alone, in the dusk, with the cleaning fluid.

SPRING COMES TO BALTIMORE

or

CHRISTMAS COMES MORE PROMPTLY

Whatever others may sing of spring,
I wish to sing there is no such thing.
Spring is simply a seasonal gap
When winter and summer overlap.
What kind of a system is it, please,
When in March you parch, and in May you freeze?
Yet give some people a glimpse of a crocus,
And all their perspective gets out of focus.
They lose their rubbers and store their V-necks,
And omit to renew their supply of Kleenex,
They shed their ulsters to walk uphill in,
And forget their sulfa and penicillin.
I suppose it's the same in Patagonia;
Today spring fever, tomorrow pneumonia.

Yes, others may sing in praise of spring,
I wish to sing there is no such thing.
Spring is a phantom, spring is a fraud,
I shall not, will not be overawed.
What if a puddle or two has thawed,
And the kittenish zephyr is velvet-pawed,
And the day is long as the night is broad,
And the robins approve and the frogs applaud,
And lovers haste to get mother-in-lawed?
I still refuse to be overawed —
Except when the clouds drift light as gossamer,

When the dogwood progresses from blossom to blos-
     somer,
And the song of the possum is nightly possumer;
Except when the rivulet sings like a dulcimer,
And the bill of fare is daily fulsomer;
When the succulent roe consoles the shad
For the offspring it never got to have had;
And the soft-shell crab finds a homey billet,
Snuggling down in a cozy skillet.

Let others refuse to sing of spring,
I wish to sing it's a splendid thing.
Let others of diet be particular,
Existing pallid and perpendicular;
We're rosy as pippins and twice as circular,
Not perpendicular, but pippindercular.
Such is spring on the generous Chesapeake,
Where recipes reach their springtime recipeake.

THERE ARE MORE WAYS TO ROAST A PIG
THAN BURNING THE HOUSE DOWN

or

YOU CAN ALWAYS STICK YOUR HEAD
IN A VOLCANO

Poring over calendars is apt to give people round
shoulders and a squint, or strabismus,

So I am perhaps fortunate in not needing a calendar
to tell me when it's my birthday or Christmas.

I know that a year has rolled around once more

When I find myself thumbing a crisp new cigarette
lighter just like the coven of other cigarette lighters
strewn on a shelf in the garage along with the
broken tire chains and the license plates for 1934.

It is only for myself that I presume to speak,

But I can light cigarettes with a cigarette lighter for
exactly one week,

And then on the eighth day something comes up for
renewal,

And sometimes it's the flint, and maybe the powder
horn or ramrod, and sometimes the fuel,

And if it's the flint you unscrew the little jigger at the
bottom and the insides jump out at you like a
jack-in-the-box and you can't get them back in
without the services of an engineer and a gunsmith
and a vet,

And if it's the fuel it gets everywhere except into the
tank and when you spin the wheel the whole thing
including your hand flares up like a crêpe Suzette.

Well, enough is enough,
And many less ingenious persons would turn to chewing
  cut plug, or sniffing snuff,
But in between birthdays and Christmases I have
  figured out a way to light cigarettes indoors and
  out in any kind of weather;
I just rub a match and a matchbox together.

SECOND LIMICK

A cook named McMurray
Got a raise in a hurry
From his Hindu employer
By favoring curry.

LINE-UP FOR YESTERDAY

AN ABC OF BASEBALL IMMORTALS

A is for Alex,
The great Alexander;
More goose eggs he pitched
Than a popular gander.

B is for Bresnahan
Back of the plate;
The Cubs were his love,
And McGraw was his hate.

C is for Cobb,
Who grew spikes and not corn,
And made all the basemen
Wish they weren't born.

D is for Dean.
The grammatical Diz,
When they asked, Who's the tops?
Said correctly, I is.

E is for Evers,
His jaw in advance;
Never afraid
To Tinker with Chance.

F is for Fordham
And Frankie and Frisch;

I wish he were back
With the Giants, I wish.

G is for Gehrig,
The pride of the Stadium;
His record pure gold,
His courage, pure radium.

H is for Hornsby;
When pitching to Rog,
The pitcher would pitch,
Then the pitcher would dodge.

I is for Me,
Not a hard-sitting man,
But an outstanding all-time
Incurable fan.

J is for Johnson.
The Big Train in his prime
Was so fast he could throw
Three strikes at a time.

K is for Keeler,
As fresh as green paint,
The fustest and mostest
To hit where they ain't.

L is Lajoie,
Whom Clevelanders love,

Napoleon himself,
With glue in his glove.

M is for Matty,
Who carried a charm
In the form of an extra
Brain in his arm.

N is for Newsom,
Bobo's favorite kin.
If you ask how he's here,
He talked himself in.

O is for Ott
Of the restless right foot.
When he leaned on the pellet,
The pellet stayed put.

P is for Plank,
The arm of the A's;
When he tangled with Matty
Games lasted for days.

Q is Don Quixote
Cornelius Mack;
Neither Yankees nor Years
Can halt his attack.

R is for Ruth.
To tell you the truth,

There's no more to be said,
Just R is for Ruth.

S is for Speaker,
Swift center-field tender;
When the ball saw him coming,
It yelled "I surrender."

T is for Terry,
The Giant from Memphis,
Whose 400 average
You can't overemphis.

U would be 'Ubbell
If Carl were a cockney;
We say Hubbell and baseball
Like football and Rockne.

V is for Vance,
The Dodgers' own Dazzy;
None of his rivals
Could throw as fast as he.

W, Wagner,
The bowlegged beauty;
Short was closed to all traffic
With Honus on duty.

X is the first
Of two x's in Foxx,

Who was right behind Ruth
With his powerful soxx.

Y is for Young
The magnificent Cy;
People batted against him,
But I never knew why.

Z is for Zenith,
The summit of fame.
These men are up there,
These men are the game.

SEPTEMBER IS SUMMER, TOO

or

IT'S NEVER TOO LATE TO BE
UNCOMFORTABLE

Well, well, well, so this is summer, isn't that mirabile
dictu,

And these are the days when whatever you sit down on
you stick to.

These are the days when those who sell four ounces of
synthetic lemonade concocted in a theater base-
ment for a quarter enter into their inheritance,

And Rum Collinses soak through paper napkins onto
people's Hepplewhites and Sheratons,

And progressive-minded citizens don their most porous
finery and frippery.

But it doesn't help, because underneath they are simultaneously sticky and slippery.

And some insomniacs woo insomnia plus pajamas and
others minus,

And everybody patronizes air-conditioned shops and
movies to get cool and then complains that the difference in temperature gives them lumbago and
sinus,

And people trapped in doorways by thunderstorms console themselves by saying, Well, anyway this will
cool it off while we wait,

So during the storm the mercury plunges from ninety-
four to ninety-three and afterwards climbs immediately to ninety-eight,

And marriages break up over such momentous questions as Who ran against Harding — Davis or Cox?
And when you go to strike a match the head dissolves on the box,
But these estival phenomena amaze me not,
What does amaze me is how every year people are amazed to discover that summer is hot.

I go to my desk to write a letter,
A simple letter without any frills;
I can't find space to write my letter,
My desk is treetop high in bills.

I got to my desk to write a poem
About a child of whom I'm afraid;
I can't get near it to write my poem
For the barrel of bills, and all unpaid.

I got to my desk for an aspirin tablet,
For a handy bottle of syrup of squills,
I reach in the drawer for the trusty bicarbonate;
My fingers fasten on nothing but bills.

I go to my desk to get my checkbook
That checks may blossom like daffodils,
Hundreds of checks to maintain my credit;
I can't get through the bills to pay my bills.

I've got more bills than there are people,
I've got bigger bills than Lincoln in bronze,
I've got older bills than a Bangor & Aroostook day
        coach,
I've got bills more quintuplicate than Dionnes.

There's a man named Slemp in Lima, Ohio,
Since 1930 he has been constantly ill,

And of all the inhabitants of this glorious nation
He is the only one who has never sent me a bill.

The trouble with bills, it costs money to pay them,
But as long as you don't, your bank is full.
I shall now save some money by opening a charge
account
With a fuller, a draper, and a carder of wool.

Kindly allow me to be your tutor.
I wish to explain about the commuter.
He rises so early and abrupt
That the robins complain he wake them upped.
Commuters think nothing could be more beautiful
Than the happy hours of the life commutiful,
But as one who tried it and now repentest,
I'd rather go twice a day to the dentist.
You struggle into the city's strife
With a shopping list from your thoughtful wife.
You repeat to yourself, as the day begins:
One charlotte russe; dozen bobby pins —
And then on the homeward trip you find
That this trifling chore has slipped your mind,
And the brilliantest explanation is useless
When you're bobby-pinless and charlotte russeless.
Let me add, to conclude this pitiful ditty,
A commuter is one who never knows how a show comes
    out because he has to leave early to catch a train
    to get him back to the country in time to catch a
    train to bring him back to the city.

THE LION

Oh, weep for Mr. and Mrs. Bryan!
He was eaten by a lion;
Following which, the lion's lioness
Up and swallowed Bryan's Bryaness.

Being a father
Is quite a bother.

You are free as air
With time to spare,

You're a fiscal rocket
With change in your pocket,

And then one morn
A child is born.

Your life has been runcible,
Irresponsible,

Like an arrow or javelin
You've been constantly travelin',

But mostly, I daresay,
Without a chaise percée,

To which by comparison
Nothing's embarison.

But all children matures,
Maybe even yours.

You improve them mentally
And straighten them dentally,

They grow tall as a lancer
And ask questions you can't answer,

And supply you with data
About how everybody else wears lipstick sooner and
    stays up later,

And if they are popular,
The phone they monopular.

They scorn the dominion
Of their parent's opinion,

They're no longer corralable
Once they find that you're fallible

But after you've raised them and educated them and
    gowned them,
They just take their little fingers and wrap you around
    them.

Being a father
Is quite a bother,
But I like it, rather.

ROLL ON, THOU DEEP AND DARK BLUE
COPY WRITER — ROLL!

GREGORY PECK
makes that
HEMINGWAY
kind of Love to
JOAN BENNETT
in "THE MACOMBER AFFAIR"

— (ADVT.)

I heard a pouting siren
Cry o'er a classic sea,
Please to remove, Lord Byron,
Your hand from off my knee!

No silver-tongued Don Juan
Shall henceforth do me wrong;
Though you sing like Mrs. Luhan,
I do not hear your song.

Go chant it to the lemming,
Go coo it to the dove;
I'm waiting for that Heming-
That Hemingway kind of love.

To think that Mr. Steinbeck
Once roused my amorous fires!
Now debutantes in Rhinebeck,
They read him to their sires.

And now my lip is bitten,
And now my heart makes moan,

To read what has been written
For Gregory and Joan.

A cinematic cordon
Is drawn around my heart,
So we'll go no more, George Gordon,
A-roving ere we part.

Though the heavens are a cup for
The pearly moon above,
Go away; I'm saving up for
That Hemingway kind of love.

EPITAPH FOR AN EXPLORER

Tiger, tiger, my mistake;
I thought that you were William Blake.

THE STRANGE CASE OF THE
ENTOMOLOGIST'S HEART

Consider the case of Mr. Suggs.

He was an eminent entomologist, which is to say he
knew nothing but bugs.

He could tell the Coleoptera from the Lepidoptera,

And the Aphidae and the Katydididae from the Grass-
hoptera.

He didn't know whether to starve a cold or feed a fever,
he was so untherapeutical,

But he knew that in 1737 J. Swammerdam's Biblia
Naturae had upset the theories of Aristotle and
Harvey by demonstrating the presence of pupal
structures under the larval cuticle.

His taste buds were such that he was always asking
dining-car stewards for their recipe for French
dressing and mayonnaise,

But he was familiar with Strauss-Durckheim's brilliant
treatise (1828) on the cockchafer and that earlier
(1760) but equally brilliant monograph on the
goat-moth caterpillar of P. Lyonnet's.

He was so unliterary that he never understood the difference between Ibid. and Anonymous,

But he spoke of 1842 as the year in which Von Kölliker
first described the formation of the blastoderm in
the egg of the midge Chironomus.

Mr. Suggs's specialty was fireflies, which he knew inside
and out and from stem to stern,

And he was on the track of why they blaze and don't
     burn,

And then one day he met a girl as fragrant as jessamine,

And he found her more fascinating than the rarest
     eleven-legged specimen,

But being a diffident swain he wished to learn how the
     land lay before burning his bridges,

So he bashfully asked her mother what she thought of
     his chances, and she encouragingly said, At sight
     of you my daughter lights up like a firefly, and
     Mr. Suggs stammered, Good gracious, what a
     strange place for a girl to light up!, and rapidly
     returned to his goat-moth caterpillars, blastoderms
     and midges.

A sea gull met an ea-gull
In an eag-loo way up North,
The sea gull eyed the ea-gull,
And the following words came forth:

I'm a sea gull, you're an ea-gull,
You are re-gull, like a king,
You are royal, like Standard Oy-al,
So how about a royal fling?

Said the sea gull to the ea-gull
It's illea-gull, but sublime,
I'm a she-gull without a he-gull,
So why are we wasting time?

Said the sea gull to the ea-gull,
I invei-gull like a dream,
I am not a squeamish sea gull,
I guarantee not to squeam.

If the wee gull turns out half ea-gull,
Don't imagine that I will fret,
Once I had one by a bea-gull,
And I haven't stopped laughing yet.

Said the ea-gull to the sea gull
As he doffed his royal crown,
You're a bad bird, you're a bad, bad bird,
But you're the only bird in town.

THIRD LIMICK

Two nudists of Dover,
Being purple all over,
Were munched by a cow
When mistaken for clover.

Some people, and it doesn't matter whether they are
    paupers or millionaires,
Think that anything they have is the best in the world
    just because it is theirs.
If they happen to own a 1921 jalopy,
They look at their neighbor's new de luxe convertible
    like the wearer of a 57th Street gown at a 14th
    Street copy.
If their seventeen-year-old child is still in the third
    grade they sneer at the graduation of the seventeen-
    year-old children of their friends,
Claiming that prodigies always come to bad ends,
And if their roof leaks,
It's because the shingles are antiques.
Other people, and it doesn't matter if they are Scan-
    dinavians or Celts,
Think that anything is better than theirs just because
    it belongs to somebody else.
If you congratulate them when their blue-blooded
    Doberman pinscher wins the obedience champion-
    ship, they look at you like a martyr,
And say that the garbage man's little Rover is really
    infinitely smarter;
And if they smoke fifteen-cent cigars they are sure
    somebody else gets better cigars for a dime.
And if they take a trip to Paris they are sure their friends
    who went to Old Orchard had a better time.

Yes, they look on their neighbor's ox and ass with
covetousness and their own ox and ass with ab-
horrence,
And if they are wives they want their husband to be
like Florence's Freddie, and if they are husbands
they want their wives to be like Freddie's Florence.
I think that comparisons are truly odious, I do not
approve of this constant proud or envious to-do;
And furthermore, dear friends, I think that you and
yours are delightful and I also think that me and
mine are delightful too.

POLTERGUEST, MY POLTERGUEST

I've put Miss Hopper upon the train,
And I hope to do so never again,
For must I do so, I shouldn't wonder
If, instead of upon it, I put her under.

Never has host encountered a visitor
Less desirabler, less exquisiter,
Or experienced such a tangy zest
In beholding the back of a parting guest.

Hoitiful-toitiful Hecate Hopper
Haunted our house and haunted it proper,
Hecate Hopper left the property
Irredeemably Hecate Hopperty.

The morning paper was her monopoly
She read it first, and Hecate Hopperly,
Handing on to the old subscriber
A wad of Dorothy Dix and fiber.

Shall we coin a phrase for "to unco-operate"?
How about trying "to Hecate Hopperate"?
On the maid's days off she found it fun
To breakfast in bed at quarter to one.

Not only was Hecate on a diet,
She insisted that all the family try it,
And all one week end we gobbled like pigs
On rutabagas and salted figs.

She clogged the pipes and she blew the fuses,
She broke the rocker that Grandma uses,
And she ran amok in the medicine chest,
Hecate Hopper, the Polterguest.

Hecate Hopper the Polterguest
Left stuff to be posted or expressed,
And also the house with a lofty look,
And a nickel, which tickled pink the cook.

If I pushed Miss Hopper under the train
I'd probably have to do it again,
For the time that I pushed her off the boat
I regretfully found Miss Hopper could float.

REPRISE

Geniuses of countless nations
Have told their love for generations
Till all their memorable phrases
Are common as goldenrod or daisies.
Their girls have glimmered like the moon,
Or shimmered like a summer noon,
Stood like lily, fled like fawn,
Now the sunset, now the dawn,
Here the princess in the tower
There the sweet forbidden flower.
Darling, when I look at you
Every aged phrase is new,
And there are moments when it seems
I've married one of Shakespeare's dreams.

I regret that before people can be reformed they have
    to be sinners,
And that before you have pianists in the family you
    have to have beginners.
When it comes to beginners' music
I take a dim viewsic.
My opinion of scales
Would not pass through the mails,
And even when listening to something called "An
    Evening in My Doll House," or "The Bee and
    the Clover,"
Why I'd like just once to hear it played all the way
    through, instead of that hard part near the end
    over and over.
Have you noticed about little fingers?
When they hit a sour note, they lingers.
And another thing about little fingers, they are always
    strawberry-jammed or cranberry-jellied-y,
And "Chopsticks" is their favorite melody,
And if there is one man who I hope his dentist was a
    sadist and all his teeth were brittle ones,
It is he who invented "Chopsticks" for the little ones.
My good wishes are less than frugal
For him who started the little ones going boogie-
    woogal,
But for him who started the little ones picking out
    "Chopsticks" on the ivories,

Well I wish him a thousand harems of a thousand wives apiece, and a thousand little ones by each wife, and each little one playing "Chopsticks" twenty-four hours a day in all the nurseries of all his harems, or wiveries.

When I a winsome babe did creep,
I'm told that I was fond of sleep,
And later, as a handsome stripling,
Gave up my life to sleep and Kipling.
At thirty, proud and in my prime,
They found me sleeping half the time,
And now that I am forty-four,
Why, sleep I doubly do adore.
As headlines range from odd to oddest
My own requirements grow more modest;
I ask no cloud of daffodils,
But just a cask of sleeping pills.
Wrapped in a robe of rosy slumber
I mock the butcher and the plumber,
A hole is dug, and in it laid
The job undone, the bill unpaid;
My young ones leap at my behest;
My waist is smaller than my chest;
I own four tires and a spare,
Besides a six-room pied-à-terre;
Europe erupts in bumper crops;
Bubble Gum King swells up and pops;
Big hussy novel wilts on cob;
In Georgia, Negro lynches mob;
The Have-nots simply love the Haves,
And people understand the Slavs;
Good fairies pay my income taxes,
And Mrs. Macy shops at Saks's.

In an era opened by mistake
I'd rather sleep than be awake.
Indeed, at times I can't recall
Why ever I wake up at all.

NOT EVEN FOR BRUNCH

When branches bend in fruitful stupor
Before the woods break out in plaid,
The super-market talks more super,
The roadside stands go slightly mad.
What garden grew this goblin harvest?
Who coined these words that strike me numb?
I will not purchase, though I starvest,
The cuke, the glad, the lope, the mum.

In happier days I sank to slumber
Murmuring names as sweet as hope:
Fair gladiolus, and cucumber,
Chrysanthemum and cantaloupe.
I greet the changelings that awoke me
With warmth a little less than luke,
As farmer and florist crowd to choke me
With glad and lope, with mum and cuke.

Go hence, far hence, you jargon-mongers,
Go soak your head in boiling ads,
Go feed to cuttlefish and congers
Your mums and lopes, your cukes and glads.
Stew in the whimsy that you dole us
I roam where magic casements ope
On cantemum spiced, and cuciolus,
On chrysanthecumber, and gladaloupe.

THE OUTCOME OF MR. BUCK'S
SUPERSTITION

Let me tell you of Aloysius Buck
Who had a pathetic belief in luck.
While the soup was waiting for him to sup
He would see a pin and pick it up.
When eating fish he toyed with the fishbones,
Making believe that they were wishbones,
And his bedside table was leaning over
Under bushel baskets of four-leafed clover.
His wife was a model of patience and tact
But at last her pleasant nature cracked.
For a birthday present he gave her a horseshoe.
She said, My dear, I'm going to divorce you.
He promised that if she'd remain Mrs. Buck
He'd never again believe in luck.
I was a fool, said Aloysius,
I'll never again be superstitious.
He brought home the blackest cats he could catch
And lit three cigarettes upon one match,
He walked his wife underneath a ladder
And often trampled on his own shadder,
And to make his un-superstition clearer
He put his foot through his wife's best mirror.
His wife was a model of patience and tact.
But at last her pleasant nature cracked
Though she liked his face and admired his carriage

She went to court and dissolved their marriage
When he said, Let's have eleven children as fast as we're
   able,
Then we can always sit down thirteen at table.

or

MR. PURVIS DREADS IT, TOO

Some say the fastest living creature is the cheetah,

Others nominate a duenna getting between a señor and
a señorita,

Which goes to show that their knowledge of natural
history is clear as a bell,

But they've never had their clothes off in a hotel.

Some hold out for the speed with which a Wagnerian
quits an opera by Puccini,

Others for the speed with which an empty stomach is
hit by a dry Martini.

These are speeds on whose superior speediness they
persistently dwell,

Which simply proves that they've never had their
clothes off in a hotel.

If you want to spite your face you can cut your nose
off,

And if you want to spite people who think that cheetahs
and duennas and dry Martinis are speedy, you
can go to a hotel and take your clothes off,

Because some people can run the hundred in ten sec-
onds and others would need only nine to circle the
earth at the equator,

And they are the ones who knock on your triple-locked
door just as you're ready for the bath and before
you can say Wait a minute! they stalk in and if

you're a man they're the maid and if you're a woman they're the waiter.

So I say Hats off to our hotel managers,

I hope they all get mistaken for Japanese beetles by scarlet tanagers,

Because there are two dubious thrills they guarantee every guest,

And one is a fleet-footed staff that laughs at locksmiths, because the other is a triple lock that will open only from the outside and only if the inmate is completely undressed.

OH SHUCKS, MA'AM, I MEAN
EXCUSE ME

The greatest error ever erred
Is a nice girl with a naughty word.
For naughty words I hold no brief,
They fill my modest heart with grief,
But since it's plainer every day,
That naughty words are here to stay,
At least let's send them back again
To where they come from: namely, men.
For men, although to language prone,
Know when to leave the stuff alone;
The stevedore, before each damn,
Stops to consider where he am;
The lumberjack is careful, too,
Of what he says in front of who;
And if surrounded by the young,
The taxi driver curbs his tongue.
The reason men speak softly thus is
That circumstances alter cusses,
And naughty words scream out like sirens
When uttered in the wrong environs.
But maidens who restrict their hips
Place no such limits on their lips;
Once they have learned a startling Verb,
No tactful qualms their heads disturb;
They scatter Adjectives hither and thence
Regardless of their audience,
And cannot hold a Noun in trust

But have to out with it, or bust,
And that's why men creep into crannies
When girls play cribbage with their grannies,
And nervous husbands develop hives
When ministers call upon their wives,
And fathers tie themselves in knots
When damsels stoop to caress their tots,
For who knows what may not be heard
From a nice girl with a naughty word?
One truth all womankind nonplusses:
That circumstances alter cusses.

Praise the spells and bless the charms,
I found April in my arms.
April golden, April cloudy,
Gracious, cruel, tender, rowdy;
April soft in flowered languor,
April cold with sudden anger,
Ever changing, ever true —
I love April, I love you.

Some of my favorite news items appear in the New
    York Herald Tribune,

A journal so nonpartisan as to be practically amphib-
    iune.

In these days when we are living on the rim of a crater

I like a paper that gets around to printing everything
    sooner or later.

Where else could I on October 2nd, 1947, have read or
    heard

That in 1929 the mockingbird was chosen by the Mis-
    sissippi Federation of Womens' Clubs to be Missis-
    sippi State bird?

Since this fact had seemingly lain dormant for seven-
    teen years before receiving mention

I naturally wondered if it had ever been brought to the
    mockingbird's attention.

I was relieved to learn from a venerable Maryland mock-
    ingbird of my acquaintance that in 1930 a notifica-
    tion ceremony was held in Jackson,

Attended by hordes of citizens, running the gamut from
    white to Protestant and Anglo-Saxon.

The mockingbirds stated that the signal honor was far
    signaler than any they had anticipated,

They had never dreamed of being Missississipated,

And then they scattered around a little suet and feed.

And voted the Mississippi Federation of Women's
    Clubs as the Federation of Women's Clubs most
    likely to succeed.

In gratitude for this information I showed my feathered
    friend an item from the same paper stating that the
    Tiber River, in Italy, is 253 miles long,
And he agreed with me when I said I wouldn't sell my
    subscription for a song.

NATURE ABHORS A VACANCY

An ordeal of which I easily tire
Is that of having a lease expire.
Where to unearth another residence?
You can't have the White House, that's the President's.
You scour the Bowery, ransack the Bronx,
Through funeral parlors and honky-tonks.
From river to river you comb the town
For a place to lay your family down.
You find one, you start to hoist your pennant,
And you stub your toe on the previous tenant.
He's in bed with croup, his children have gout,
And you can't push in until they pull out,
And when they pull out, the painters take on
And your date with the movers has come and gone,
So your furniture in storage sits
While you camp out royally at the Ritz.
When leases expire, one wish I've got,
To be a landlord, and live on a yacht.

LINES TO BE EMBROIDERED ON A BIB

or

THE CHILD IS FATHER OF THE MAN, BUT NOT FOR QUITE A WHILE

So Thomas Edison
Never drank his medicine;
So Blackstone and Hoyle
Refused cod-liver oil;
So Sir Thomas Malory
Never heard of a calory;
So the Earl of Lennox
Murdered Rizzio without the aid of vitamins or calis-
    thenox;
So Socrates and Plato
Ate dessert without finishing their potato;
So spinach was too spinachy
For Leonardo da Vinaci;
Well, it's all immaterial,
So eat your nice cereal,
And if you want to name your own ration,
First go get a reputation.

FOURTH LIMICK

Three young Tennesseans
Whom snobs called plebeians
Cried, What do you mean?
We's married to we-uns.

How wise I am to have instructed the butler to instruct
  the first footman to instruct the second footman
  to instruct the doorman to order my carriage;
I am about to volunteer a definition of marriage.
Just as I know that there are two Hagens, Walter and
  Copen,
I know that marriage is a legal and religious alliance
  entered into by a man who can't sleep with the
  window shut and a woman who can't sleep with
  the window open,
Also he can't sleep until he has read the last hundred
  pages to find out whether his suspicions of the
  murdered eccentric recluse's avaricious secretary
  were right,
And she can't sleep until he puts out the light,
Which when he finally does she is still awake and turns
  on hers,
And if he thinks she's going to turn it off before she
  finds out whether Janis marries the shy young
  clergyman or the sophisticated polo player, he
  errs.
Moreover just as I am unsure of the difference between
  flora and fauna and flotsam and jetsam
I am quite sure that marriage is the alliance of two
  people one of whom never remembers birthdays
  and the other never forgetsam,
And the one refuses to believe there is a leak in the

water pipe or the gas pipe and the other is con-
vinced she is about to asphyxiate or drown,

And the other says Quick get up and get my hairbrushes
off the window sill, it's raining in, and the one re-
plies Oh they're all right, it's only raining straight
down.

That is why marriage is so much more interesting than
divorce,

Because it's the only known example of the happy meet-
ing of the immovable object and the irresistible
force.

So I hope husbands and wives will continue to debate
and combat over everything debatable and com-
batable,

Because I believe a little incompatibility is the spice
of life, particularly if he has income and she is
pattable.

If I have one outstanding desire
It is to know the answer to the question, Where's the
    fire?
Shall I tell you about my environs?
They are populated exclusively by alarums and sirens.
No wonder I flunked my secret agent course, when
    every time I tackled my cipher and code work,
Why, along came some hook-and-ladder on its road
    work.
The engines hoot by, a dozen times per diem,
And to me it's Mysterious, and Mysterious with a big
    M, not a wee m,
Because no matter how desperately I try to,
I can never spot hide or hair of the fires they are hoot-
    ing by to.
I am dazed, please do not criticize my daze;
I guess I have heard a million fire engines hoot by, yet
    I have never seen so much as a doghouse ablaze.
Firemen, what is your destination?
Is there really a conflagration?
You have lickety-splitted by so often that my thoughts
    are utterly split-licketed;
I don't believe there ever was a fire, I believe I'm just
    being picketed.

Autumn to some is mellowly fruitful,
Autumn to others is disreputeful.
In autumn in Boston and Butte and Stamford
Winter suits are un-mothballed and woolies un-
　　camphored,
And you find, as you haul them out of the trunk,
Either you have swollen or they have shrunk.
Your overcoat now fills you with doubt of it;
You're too warm in it, and too cold out of it.
Now flies are dead as Egyptian queens,
So you mash your thumbs taking out the screens;
You put the storm windows on, and then
The flies all come to life again.
And look at the days, how autumn has shortened 'em.
Some people like autumn. Well, autumn or autn'tumn?

Whales have calves,
Cats have kittens,
Bears have cubs,
Bats have bittens.
Swans have cygnets,
Seals have puppies,
But guppies just have little guppies.

My grandpa wasn't salty,
No hero he of fable,
His English wasn't faulty,
He wore a coat at table.
His character lacked the color
Of either saint or satyr,
His life was rather duller
Than that of Walter Pater.

Look at Grandpa, take a look!
How can I write a book!

His temper wasn't crusty,
He shone not forth majestic
For barroom exploits lusty,
Or tyranny domestic.
He swung not on the gallows
But went to his salvation
While toasting stale marshmallows,
His only dissipation.

Look at Grandpa, take a look!
How can I write a book!

My Uncle John was cautious,
He never slipped his anchor,
His probity was nauseous,
In fact he was a banker.

He hubbed no hubba hubbas,
And buckled he no swashes,
He wore a pair of rubbers
Inside of his galoshes.

Look at my uncle, take a look!
How can I write a book!

My other uncle, Herbie,
Just once enlarged his orbit,
The day he crushed his derby
While cheering James J. Corbett.
No toper he, or wencher,
He backed nor horse nor houri,
His raciest adventure
A summons to the jury.

Look at my uncles, take a look! ·
How can I write a book!

Round my ancestral menfolk
There hangs no spicy aura,
I have no racy kinfolk
From Rome or Gloccamora.
Not nitwits, not Napoleons,
The mill they were the run of,
My family weren't Mongolians;
Then whom can I make fun of?

Look!
No book!

IS TOMORROW REALLY ANOTHER DAY?

or

NO MORE OF THE SAME, PLEASE

This is the day when all the oaks are turning into acorns
    instead of acorns into oaks,
The day I would cheer myself with jokes.
This is the day when there is nothing at the movies but
    the Ritz Brothers and the chicken has no white
    meat and the asparagus no tips,
The day I would console myself with quips.
This is the day when the stomach revolves at the thought
    of a coddled egg and the radio assails the ear with
    zesty tangs and tangy zests,
The day I would play with my fingers and hearten my-
    self with jests.
This is the day when everybody is feeling better than
    me no matter where I traipse,
The day I would resurrect myself with japes.
This is the day when were I an ancient Briton I would
    paint my face not with bright blue woad but with
    pale woad,
The day I would wake my spirit with wit and waggery,
    and the best I can do is wonder if Mark, or Steam-
    boat Twain, ever met that equally well-known
    Twain, Wailwoad.
This is, ah, this is the day
When if the Corn Exchange Bank should cash my
    check in corn instead of cash I could only murmur,
    Well it ain't hay.

This is the day when kind words are more than coro-
nets and unkind words more than mayhem,
The day I hope to get to bed today in the P.M., not
tomorrow in the A.M.

A prepared position Man hankers for
Is parallel to, and above the floor,
For thither retreating horizontally
He evades the issues that charge him frontally.
But pumpkins do not burgeon in Maytime,
And bed is out of bounds in daytime.
A man in pajamas after nine
Transgresses the housewife's Party Line.
He's unethical and unpatriotic,
Unkempt, uncouth, unaristocrotic,
Unwept, unhonored, unsung, unread,
And, if he doesn't get up, unfed.
That is why he smiles when the moment comes
When hands are hot and forehead hums,
When throat is parched and nostrils rankle
And legs are aching from knee to ankle.
Making sure the housewife observes his plight,
He bravely whispers he's quite all right,
What's a spot of fever, a spell of dizziness.
Where's his hat, he is off to business.
So she telephones the office for him,
And stoups of lemonade doth pour him,
And trees his shoes and hangs his clothes up
And introduces drops his nose up,
She fetches toast as light as froth,
And bouillon, consommé and broth,
And be he Harvardite or Yaleite,
She orders him to bed by daylight,

Like Heaven chastening a Baalite
She orders him to bed by daylight.
Beneath the sheets he cracks his knuckles
And chokes to cover up his chuckles,
And coughs a spirited cadenza
In grateful praise of influenza.

GOOD RIDDANCE, BUT NOW WHAT?

Come children, gather round my knee;
Something is about to be.

Tonight's December thirty-first,
Something is about to burst.

The clock is crouching, dark and small,
Like a time bomb in the hall.

Hark, it's midnight, children dear.
Duck! Here comes another year!

IS THIS SEAT TAKEN? YES

or

MY NECK IS STICKING IN

I hope that in my eldering age I'm not becoming notice-
    ably querulous,
But I feel that conversations with strangers can be
    perilous.
Consider the case of the two strangers who met in a
    hotel dining room in Alabama,
And the menu was rather less than a panorama,
Indeed, it was as repetitious as a snore,
And the first stranger said, I'm a little sick of corn pone,
    and the second stranger, who was tall, tan, and tur-
    baned, said, Glad to know you, I'm Mohammed
    Khan, a big Sikh of Cawnpore.
Then take the two strangers who met at a Harvard class
    reunion,
One was a Bostonian and the other was an Altoonian,
And the first stranger said, Why are you taking notes,
    are you the official annotator?
And the second stranger said, I am noting the difference
    between Fulton Lewis Jr. and a pomme soufflé,
    Fulton Lewis Jr. is just a commentator but a pomme
    soufflé is a veritable coloratura-soprana tater.
I am also disturbed by accounts of the two strangers,
    one male and one female, who met on the banks of
    the Congo and shared a bowl of semolina,
And presently he said, You've got eyes like a gazelle,

and she giggled and said, Eyes like a gazelle? And
he said, No, you's like a hyena.
This is the sort of experience for which I do not hanker,
So if you will excuse me, I shall now run over to the
Banker's Trust Company and trust a banker.

In between the route marks
And the shaving rhymes,
Black and yellow markers
Comment on the times.

All along the highway
Hear the signs discourse:

MEN
SLOW
WORKING

;

SADDLE
CROSSING
HORSE

.

Cryptic crossroad preachers
Proffer good advice,
Helping wary drivers
Keep out of Paradise.

Transcontinental sermons,
Transcendental talk:

SOFT
CAUTION
SHOULDERS

;

CROSS

CHILDREN

WALK

·

Wisest of their proverbs,
Truest of their talk,
Have I found that dictum:

CROSS

CHILDREN

WALK

·

When Adam took the highway
He left his sons a guide:

CROSS

CHILDREN

WALK

;

CHEERFUL

CHILDREN

RIDE

·

HAVE YOU TRIED STAYING AWAKE?

or

THEY'LL FIND A WAY TO STOP THAT, TOO

Most people's downy couches have a footboard and a
    headboard,
And some people's downy couches also have a bed-
    board.
I must tell you before I forgets
That a bed-board is different from a bed and board,
    which is what when your wife leaves it you are no
    longer responsible for her debts,
But if you can't get to sleep because your couch is so
    downy that you wallow and roll like a tug-boat off
    Cape Hatteras,
Why, you make it un-downy by slipping a bed-board
    under your matteras,
Thereby earning, whether you wear pajamas or a gown,
The unusual privilege of getting to sleep by walking the
    plank lying down.
O Civilization, O Progress, O Human Ingenuity!
O Fatuity in Perpetuity!
One genius chooses downy couches to set his mind
    upon,
And he spends a lifetime tinkering with Angeldust and
    Fogfoam and Bubblemist until he has invented the
    downiest couch ever reclined upon,
Whereupon another genius immediately invents a slab
    of wood that you can put under it to harden it,

And up-and-coming dealers may now feature the most irresistible of downy couches and the most immovable of bed-boards simultaneously, like the poison bottle with the antidote on the label, so if I giggle in my hammock I hope you will pardon it.

1

Walter Savage Landor
Stood before the fire of life with candor.
Coventry Patmore
Sat more.

2

Robert Browning
Avoided drowning,
Unparallelly
To P. B. Shelley.

3

Robert Herrick
Was an odd sort of cleric.
Another one
Was John Donne.

4

Charles Algernon Swinburne
Glowed less with sunburn than with ginburn.
Alfred Lord Tennyson
Settled for venison.

5

Did Dryden
Predecease Haydn?
Or did Haydn
Predecease Dryden?
When it comes to dates
I'm at sevens and eights.

OTHERS IN THE CAST INCLUDE

A rose is a rose is a rose, and a caterpillar is a tractor,

And an actor is an actor is an actor.

Not only is an actor an actor an actor, but he is also a
martyr a martyr,

Because he is persecuted by playwrights, from Saroyan
to Sartre,

Because as certain as Sardi's or Max Factor,

The playwright gives all the best lines to some other
actor,

So all our actor gets to say is, "I love you, Miss Scarlett,
'deed I do,"

While the other actor gets to say, "It's hell's fire in my
veins, this desperate thirst for you."

Even life itself plays cruel tricks on actors, and nobody
cares,

As in the recent case of Jackie Cooper, who when his
house was set afire by lightning lowered his wife
from the window on knotted sheets and slid down
himself, only to be greeted on the lawn by his
mother-in-law, who had walked downstairs.

THE ASP

Whenever I behold an asp
I can't suppress a prudish gasp.
I do not charge the asp with matricide,
But what about his Cleopatricide?

HOW THE RHINOCEROS GOT ITS HIDE

or

THE CONFESSIONS OF COUNT MOWGLI DE SADE

A child is naturally of a green age,
And this child, the earliest possible teen age;
It might be Gretel, it might be Hansel,
And it lies in bed with an active tonsil.
It surveys the ceiling with all the boredom
That distinguishes Truman Capote from Fordham.
You exert your wits and cudgel your powers
To enliven its laggard and aching hours.
When your ingenuity starts to grovel
You hope it might like to read a novel;
You think as you tiptoe away from the cot
You'll give it a book, but which or what?
Well, something with horses
Instead of divorces,
Or Doberman pinschers
Instead of wenchers,
Or Fuzzy Wuzzies
Instead of hussies,
Alarms and excursions
Instead of perversions,
With heroes of whiloms
Instead of asylums,
Desert isles
Instead of necrophiles,
Or alligators

Instead of satyrs,
Even debutantes debbing
Instead of Krafft-Ebing,
So you turn to your favorite book reviewer,
Whose mind is matiewer
As well as piewer,
A permanent, eminent publishers'-tea lion,
And he recommends something about a sea lion,
And the sea lion loves a lovable lad,
An urchin, a gamin, a tyke, a tad,
Who romps with his amphibious pal
Through an Oz-like valley in Southern Cal.,
A tale like a draught from an oaken dipper,
Tom Sawyer and Huckleberry Flipper.
You accept his word and deliver the book
Without first taking a cautious look.
Not until it's been studied a week or two
Do you pick it up to leaf it through.
It opens as if by the finger of fate,
Or magic, at page two-ninety-eight.
But where is the sea lion? Where's the lad?
The piscivorous clown and the doting tad?
Shiver your timbers and blast your binnacle!
It's a kissless bride and her symptoms clinical,
And the details her doctor has to go on
Are distinctly et cetera and so on.
May Pulitzer maul you, you old reviewer!
Everything goes in literatiewer,
But when a person is personally responsible

For the reading of a younger person still adenoidable
and tonsible,
Why not be just a little benignal
And hoist a friendly warning signal?
I hope all your children are mermaids, I wist,
And they all marry sea lions and don't get kissed.

I don't want to be classed among the pedantics,

But next time I visit friends who have moved to the
    country I want to get together with them on
    terminology, or semantics.

When you ask them on the telephone how to get there
    they smilingly cry that it is simple,

In fact you can practically see them dimple,

You just drive on Route 402 to Hartley and then bear
    left a couple of miles till you cross a stream,

Which they imply is alive with tench, chub, dace, ide,
    strugeon and bream,

And you go on till you reach the fourth road on the
    right,

And you can't miss their house because it is on a rise
    and it is white.

Well it's a neighborhood of which you have never been
    a frequenter,

But you start out on 402 and soon find yourself trying
    to disentangle Hartley from East Hartley, West
    Hartley, North and South Hartley, and Hartley
    Center,

And you bear left a couple of miles peering through
    the windshield, which is smattered with gnats and
    midges,

And suddenly the road is alive with bridges,

And your tires begin to scream

As you try to decide which bridge spans a rill, which a

run, which a branch, which a creek, which a brook or river, and which presumably a stream;

And having passed this test you begin to count roads on the right, than which no more exhausting test is to be found,

For who is to say which is a road, which a lane, which a driveway and which just a place where somebody backed in to turn around?

But anyhow turning around seems a good idea so there is one thing I don't know still:

Whether that white house where the cocktails are getting warm and the dinner cold is on a ridge, a ledge, a knoll, a rise, or a hill.

HE DIGS, HE DUG, HE HAS DUG

Say not Eve needed Adam's pardon
For their eviction from the Garden;
I only hope some power divine
Gets round to ousting me from mine.
On bended knee, perspiring clammily,
I scrape the soil to feed my family,
Untaught, unteachable, undramatic,
A figure sorry and sciatic.
I brood as patiently as Buddha,
Nothing comes up the way it shuddha.
They're making playshoes of my celery,
It's rubbery, and purple-yellery,
My beets have botts, my kale has hives,
There's something crawly in my chives,
And jeering insects think it cute
To swallow my spray and spit out my fruit.
My garden will never make me famous,
I'm a horticultural ignoramus,
I can't tell a stringbean from a soybean,
Or even a girl bean from a boy bean.

THE ETERNAL VERNAL

or

IN ALL MY DREAMS MY FAIR FACE BEAMS

Forgive this singsong,
It's just my spring song.
All winter like the blossoms
I've been playing possums,
But with April adjacent
I'm a possum renascent.
I'm the Renaissance
In gabardine pants,
I'm a gossoon once more,
Not forty-five, but forty-four,
I drink my kumiss
With pepper and pumice,
I swim where the herring do
In search of derring-do,
I crouch in a pergola
To catch me a burgola,
I'm Gustavus Adolphus
Among tennis players and golphus,
Compared to me they're a tortoise
With advanced rigor mortis,
I combine the music of Götterdämmerung
With the words of the Decamerrung,
I woo nymphs like billy-o
With my well-known punctilio,
Which unless I've progressed

· 136 ·

Is the punkest tilio by actual test,
I roll a one and a two at dice and consider them better
    than a good cook or a good wife are,
Because one and two is free, and that's what the best
    things in life are,
And if anyone disagrees they might just as well not have
    done it,
Because I know this business backwards and that's the
    way I propose to run it.
In a word, it is spring,
And I can do any thing.

Brother, do you belong to an exclusive fraternity? Sister,
     are you high up in an exclusive sorority?

I recommend to you a recent advertisement tersely and
     tastefully entitled "The Cigarette of the Minority."

Brothers and Sisters, are you socially honest-to-God one
     hundred per cent crème de la crème?

The copy-writer says, "Virginia Rounds are expressly
     created for that limited audience which makes a
     sharp distinction between what does for everybody
     and what is acceptable to them."

Let us absently whistle a snatch from the "Horst
     Wessel Song" as we try to remember where we
     have previously glimpsed that limited audience's
     face;

Perhaps when it was voting dry because Prohibition got
     the workingman to work on time, but limited
     audiences who could sleep late could stay up till
     dawn over pinch-bottle Scotch at $120 a case,

Or, to take a select journey through time and space,

Surely we saw it recently at Voisin when a faultlessly
     tailored gentleman turned to the faultlessly jeweled
     dowager which had just slipped a crisp new check
     into his pocket and murmured between mouthfuls
     of Steak Béarnaise, "The trouble with a democ-
     racy is that the lower classes don't know their
     place."

Here is, we are assured, "A cigarette for those who make

a cult of doing all things better, particularly when the better costs so little more,"

So how is your cult life, friends, and what the hell do you think that wad on your hip is for?

And do not overlook the fact, hoch-geboren Bretheren and Sisteren, that "Smart folk to whom you offer a Virginia Round know they cost a little more," which leads me, as a Lucky Striker,

Whenever I offer smart folk a Lucky to also slip them a nickel for themselves, just to show I am not a piker.

I rise to salute the feminine sex
You never know what they're up to nex.
You never can tell if a lady is going
To rock a cradle or build a Boeing.
One moment she's cooking her husband's dinner,
The next, she's riding the Preakness winner.
At five she punctures an enemy sniper,
And at six she's folding the baby's diper,
But running for Congress or brewing a chowder
She still depends on her paint and powder.
Bless all the ladies, from shrew to saint,
And bless their powder and bless their paint,
But I'd like their lipstick even finer
Upon their lips, not upon the china.
I'm weary of lipstick on rims of glasses,
Lipstick on teacups and demitasses,
Lipstick on tumblers and soup tureens,
On the morning paper, on magazines.
I love to look at the feminine sex,
But I can't, I've got lipstick on my specs.

FIFTH LIMICK

A young flirt of Ceylon,
Who led the boys on,
Playing Follow the Leda
Succumbed to a swan.

COUSIN EUPHEMIA KNOWS BEST

or

PHYSICIAN, HEAL SOMEBODY ELSE

Some people don't want to be doctors because they
    think doctors don't make a good living,

And also get called away from their bed at night and
    from their dinner on Christmas and Thanksgiving,

And other people don't want to be doctors because a
    doctor's friends never take their symptoms to his
    office at ten dollars a throw but insert them into
    a friendly game of gin rummy or backgammon,

And ask questions about their blood count just as the
    doctor is lining up an elusive putt or an elusive
    salmon.

These considerations do not influence me a particle;

I do not want to be a doctor simply because somewhere
    in the family of every patient is a female who has
    read an article.

You remove a youngster's tonsils and the result is a
    triumph of medical and surgical science,

He stops coughing and sniffling and gains eleven
    pounds and gets elected captain of the Junior
    Giants,

But his great-aunt spreads the word that you are a
    quack,

Because she read an article in the paper last Sunday
    where some Rumanian savant stated that tonsil-
    lectomy is a thing of the past and the Balkan hospi-

tals are bulging with people standing in line to
have their tonsils put back.
You suggest calamine lotion for the baby's prickly heat,
And you are at once relegated to the back seat,
Because its grandmother's cousin has seen an article in
the "Household Hints" department of Winning
Parcheesi that says the only remedy for prickly
heat is homogenized streptomycin,
And somebody's sister-in-law has seen an article where
the pathologist of Better Houses and Trailers says
calamine lotion is out, a conscientious medicine
man wouldn't apply calamine lotion to an itching
bison.
I once read an unwritten article by a doctor saying
there is only one cure for a patient's female relative
who has read an article:
A hatpin in the left ventricle of the hearticle.

Have you bought a suit at Spand and Spitz?
They won't let you wear it unless it fits.
That's what they warn you in all their ads,
And Spand and Spitz are scrupulous lads.
Spand and Spitz are intensely scrupulous,
You can't wear their suit if the seat is droopulous.
Do you want it for slumming, or tea at the Ritz?
They won't let you wear it unless it fits.
The suit you're wearing could not be elder,
You've promised it to a needy welder,
The sleeves are shiny, the derrière splits,
So you choose a new one at Spand and Spitz.
The pants they carry are envy arousers,
In fact, they are not pants, they are trousers.
You select a suit and you call it quits,
As far as you are concerned, it fits.
You put your money and keys and comb in it,
You prepare to pay, and walk on home in it,
When here comes Spitz and here comes Spand,
They look at you like a swollen gland,
Spitz swears to Spand, who swears to Spitz,
They won't let you wear it unless it fits.
You adore the suit, you appeal to Spand,
He jerks it apart with loving hand;
You wish to wear it, you cry to Spitz,
He rips it off, while Spand on you sits.
It may be the suit that you're who it's made for,
The suit you have fought and bought and paid for;

But if Spand and Spitz don't admit it fits you,
To wear it away, you must learn jujitsu.
The hell with this esthetic palaver
When you just want to cover your threadbare cadaver.

June means weddings in everyone's lexicon,
Weddings in Swedish, weddings in Mexican.
Breezes play Mendelssohn, treeses play Youmans,
Birds wed birds, and humans wed humans.
All year long the gentlemen woo,
But the ladies dream of a June "I do."
Ladies grow loony, and gentlemen loonier;
This year's June is next year's Junior.

Newspapermen say that of all work, newspaper work is
the infernalist,
But nevertheless I am studying up to be a journalist.
I do not aspire to be a Pearson or a Pegler or a Gunther,
I don't think I will ever be selected as a Book-of-the-
Monther,
I don't hope to score any scoops or beat any deadlines,
But after a careful 10-year examination of the press I
do think I have caught the knack of writing face-
tious little headlines.
Suppose a marmoset escapes in a saloon and mingles
with the imbibers,
Why, "Monkey Business" is the heading expected by
the subscribers,
And when a steer escapes on the way to the slaughter-
house and is recaptured by a cowboy from Madison
Square Garden my cup is doubly full,
Because then I can write either "A Bum Steer" or
"Throwing the Bull."
What can be apter than "Fowl Play" when the minis-
ter's Rhode Island Reds disappear at dawn,
Or be it Mrs. Somebody-or-other's of 13 South Water
Street's amorous Pekinese that is missing, what
could be more appropriate than "Dog-Gone"?
My, my, in the names of animals how many cryptic
little giggles are hidden;
Which of you could guess what type of creature is re-
ferred to in items entitled "A Cat-astrophe" or

"Poor Fish" or "Gets Farmer's Goat," or "No
Kiddin' "?
No, I may never win any prizes from Mr. Pulitzer,
But when it comes to supplying the customers with
little jokes for their breakfast table I will always be
in there pitching honestly and trulitzer.

FIRST CHILD . . . SECOND CHILD

FIRST

Be it a girl, or one of the boys,
It is scarlet all over its avoirdupois,
It is red, it is boiled; could the obstetrician
Have possibly been a lobstertrician?
His degrees and credentials were hunky-dory,
But how's for an infantile inventory?
Here's the prodigy, here's the miracle!
Whether its head is oval or spherical,
You rejoice to find it has only one,
Having dreaded a two-headed daughter or son;
Here's the phenomenon all complete,
It's got two hands, it's got two feet,
Only natural, but pleasing, because
For months you have dreamed of flippers or claws.
Furthermore, it is fully equipped:
Fingers and toes with nails are tipped;
It's even got eyes, and a mouth clear cut;
When the mouth comes open the eyes go shut,
When the eyes go shut the breath is loosed
And the presence of lungs can be deduced.
Let the rockets flash and the cannon thunder,
This child is a marvel, a matchless wonder.
A staggering child, a child astounding,
Dazzling, diaperless, dumfounding,
Stupendous, miraculous, unsurpassed,
A child to stagger and flabbergast,
Bright as a button, sharp as a thorn,
And the only perfect one ever born.

SECOND

Arrived this evening at half-past nine.
Everybody is doing fine.
Is it a boy, or quite the reverse?
You can call in the morning and ask the nurse.

IT LOOKS LIKE SNOW

or

MY LIFE IN GALOSHES

Some people are dipsomaniacs,
And other people are Calypsomaniacs,
And in my heart both kinds occupy the front row
Compared to the aficionados of snow.
How like taxes is snow on doorstep and lawn!
How rapidly imposed, how reluctantly withdrawn!
And how indestructible, because unless it melts,
Every shovelful you take from one place you just have
      to put it some place else.
And how otherwise I gaze at it than stout Cortez
      gazing at the Pacific or stout Columbus gazing at
      a San Dominigan,
Because Columbus and Cortez never had to drive from
      an ice-capped byway onto a well-cleared highway
      and hear their chains chattering, Off agin, on
      agin, your fender is gone agin, Finnegan.
Snow differs from rain because rain is wet and snow is
      clammy,
And it never rains but it pours and it never snows but
      either the night you were going to the theater or
      some friends you particularly detest have just left
      for Miami.
Children like snow, which still leaves my point far from
      moot,
Because children also like bubble gum and listening to

radio mysteries while they are doing their square
root,
So when our incorporated young place an order for
snow I suggest that their parents form into We-
countermands-it companies,
Because there is only one thing I like about snow
which is that transit companies hate it, and I hate
transit companies.

CONFESSION TO BE TRACED ON A
BIRTHDAY CAKE

Lots of people are richer than me,
Yet pay a slenderer tax;
Their Paragraph Sevens yearly wane
As their Paragraph Sixes wax.
Lots of people have stocks and bonds
To further their romances;
I've cashed my ultimate Savings Stamp —
But nobody else has Frances.

Lots of people are stronger than me,
And greater athletic menaces;
They poise like gods on diving boards
And win their racquets and tennises.
Lots of people have lots more grace
And cut fine figures at dances,
While I was born with galoshes on —
But nobody else has Frances.

Lots of people are wiser than me,
And carry within their cranium
The implications of Stein and Joyce
And the properties of uranium.
They know the mileage to every star
In the heaven's vast expanses;
I'm inclined to believe that the world is flat —
But nobody else has Frances.

Speaking of wisdom and wealth and grace —
As recently I have dared to —
There are lots of people compared to whom
I'd rather not be compared to.
There are people I ought to wish I was;
But under the circumstances,
I prefer to continue my life as me —
For nobody else has Frances.

I like to think about that great French critic and his-
     torian, Hippolyte Adolphe Taine.
I like to think about his great French critical and his-
     torical brain.
He died in 1893 at the age of sixty-five,
But previously he had been alive.
He wrote many books of outstanding worth,
But this was before his death, although following his
     birth.
He tried to interpret human culture in terms of outer
     environment,
And he knew exactly what the biographers of Rousseau
     and Shelley and Lord Byron meant.
His great philosophical work, De l'intelligence, in
     which he connected physiology with psychology,
     was written after meeting a girl named Lola,
And greatly influenced the pens of Flaubert, de Mau-
     passant, and Zola.
He did much to establish positivism in France,
And his famous History of English Literature was writ-
     ten on purpose and not by chance.
Yes, Hippolyte Adolphe Taine may have been only five
     foot three, but he was a scholar of the most dis-
     cerning;
Whereas his oafish brother Casimir, although he stood
     six foot seven in his bobby-socks, couldn't spell
     C–H–A–T, cat, and was pointed at as the long
     Taine that had no learning.

How many gifted pens have penned
That Mother is a boy's best friend!·
How many more with like afflatus
Award the dog that honored status!
I hope my tongue in prune juice smothers
If I belittle dogs or mothers,
But gracious, how can I agree?
I know my own best friend is Me.
We share our joys and our aversions,
We're thicker than the Medes and Persians,
We blend like voices in a chorus,
The same things please, the same things bore us.
If I am broke, then Me needs money;
I make a joke, Me finds it funny.
I think of bees, Me shares the craving;
If I have whiskers, Me needs shaving.
I know what I like, Me knows what art is;
We hate the people at cocktail parties,
When I can stand the crowd no more,
Why, Me is halfway to the door.
We two reactionary codgers
Prefer the Giants to the Dodgers,
I am a dodo; Me, an auk;
We grieve that pictures learned to talk;
For every sin that I produce
Kind Me can find some soft excuse,
And when I blow a final gasket,
Who but Me will share my casket?

Beside us, Pythias and Damon
Were just two unacquainted laymen.
Sneer not, for if you answer true,
Don't you feel that way about You?

December twenty-fourth is an exciting day because it is
the day before Christmas; but December twenty-
sixth is a dreary day because it is the day after,

And people don't even want to take their heads out
from under the covers unless they hafter.

December twenty-fifth is an exciting day because it is
what people refer to when Merry Christmas they
wish you;

But December twenty-sixth is just the day you spend
tripping over ribbons and wading through green
and scarlet tissue.

It is a day of such anticlimax as to frustrate the most
ambitious,

It is lined with gray satin like a medium-priced casket,
its atmosphere is faintly morticious.

It is a day oppressive as asthma,

A day on which you want to call up the blood bank and
ask them to return your plasma.

It is a day of headaches that set you sighing with nos-
talgia

For your old neuralgia.

Its hours are as dilatory

As a 10-cent depilatory.

Indeed it is a day subject to such obsecration and
obloquy

That I am beginning to feel sorry for it, my knees are
getting wobloquy as I strangle a sobloquy.

I am regretful that in discussing the reputation of December twenty-sixth I may have said anything to jeopardize it,

So by way of making amends I suggest that from now on we not necessarily lionize it, but couldn't we maybe just leopardize it?

THE MIDDLE

When I remember bygone days
I think how evening follows morn;
So many I loved were not yet dead,
So many I love were not yet born.

FOR A GOOD DOG

My little dog ten years ago
Was arrogant and spry,
Her backbone was a bended bow
For arrows in her eye.
Her step was proud, her bark was loud,
Her nose was in the sky,
But she was ten years younger then,
And so, by God, was I.

Small birds on stilts along the beach
Rose up with piping cry,
And as they flashed beyond her reach
I thought to see her fly.
If natural law refused her wings,
That law she would defy,
For she could hear unheard-of things,
And so, at times, could I.

Ten years ago she split the air
To seize what she could spy;
Tonight she bumps against a chair,
Betrayed by milky eye.
She seems to pant, Time up, time up!
My little dog must die,
And lie in dust with Hector's pup;
So, presently, must I.

Once there was a man named Mr. Farr,

And he dreamed he had a wife who summer or winter
didn't make him close the window when she got
in the car.

If he inadvertently ran through a red light she made no
remark,

And she never told him where and how to park.

When he was sad she was silent and when he was cheery
she was cheerier,

And if the Smiths drove to the seashore in two hours via
Route 212 and he insisted on Route 176 and took
three hours she found Route 176 infinitely superior.

When he came home in the rain she had a hot bath
drawn for his arrival,

And if she wanted to see the new Boyer picture and he
wanted the old Marx Brothers picture, they saw the
revival.

Although she didn't smoke she had ashtrays everywhere,
but if he dropped ashes on the floor she wasn't
critical or heckly,

And during baseball broadcasts she didn't talk, she kept
score, and correckly.

She provided him with unscented soap,

And greeted his feeblest jest like a studio audience greet-
ing a mention of Hope by Crosby or Crosby by
Hope.

You understand that Mr. Farr was a bachelor,

And to a bachelor such dreams come nachelor.

THE PERFECT HUSBAND

He tells you when you've got on
    too much lipstick,
And helps you with your girdle
    when your hips stick.

Now elbow-deep in middle age,
A viewer I'm of video,
And some of it is beautiful,
But most of it is hideo.

I like to view the video
On Saturdays, for instance.
I like to cheer the Notre Dames,
The Rutgerses and Princetons.

I like to view Citation run,
I like to view his jockey,
I like to view the baseball game,
I like to view the hockey.

But there are less exalted scenes
I view upon the video,
The lady wrestlers make me sick.
Perhaps I'm too fastideo.

And evening vaudevideo,
I view it with alarum,
I can't determine which it's for,
The nursery or the barum.

Yet ask me to your house to view,
And I'll be there immidiate,
For all the world is video,
And I the village videot.

INDEX OF FIRST LINES